TENNIS
FOR
BEGINNERS

TENNIS
FOR
BEGINNERS

BY LUD DUROSKA

CONSULTANT:
CHARLES LUNDGREN

INTRODUCTION BY
JIMMY CONNORS

GROSSET & DUNLAP
PUBLISHERS   NEW YORK

Library of Congress Catalog Card Number 74-94
ISBN: 0-448-11792-4 (Trade Edition)
ISBN: 0-448-13236-2 (Library Edition)
Copyright © 1975 by Lud Duroska.
All rights reserved.
Published simultaneously in Canada.
Printed in the United States of America.

CONTENTS

INTRODUCTION

There's only one way I know how to play tennis—and that is to win. Every time I step onto a court for a match, I have to believe that I can beat the other guy. Of course, that hasn't always happened. But I think having a positive attitude toward tennis—and most things in life—is the way you can accomplish more.

I was lucky to be born into a family where my mother and my grandmother had played the game, so I was swinging a racquet when I was three years old. There never was any doubt in my mind while I was growing up concerning what

I wanted to be: the best tennis player in the world. I moved to California when I was 15 in order to take lessons from Pancho Segura, and nobody could count the hours that we spent together as he taught me so much about the game. He was a marvelous teacher and I will always be grateful to him.

Most of you reading this book are just beginning to learn how to play and don't plan on making it a career. That's fine. Tennis is also a fun sport and you can get a lot of pleasure out of it competing with friends and finding out who is the local king of the hill. Since tennis is an individual sport, it's all up to you how much you get out of it. There are no substitutes for staying in condition, practicing hard, and concentrating on your strokes.

As I like to say: "Move your feet like crazy and be able to relax"—and you'll win more than your share of the points. Good luck.

Jimmy Connors

Jimmy Connors became the No. 1 player in the tennis world in 1974 when he captured the two most prestigious singles championships—Wimbledon and the United States Open. In July he decisively defeated veteran Ken Rosewall of Australia in the Wimbledon final, 6-1, 6-1, 6-4. Two months later (and only eight days after his twenty-second birthday), he capped his triumphant progress to the United States title by again conquering Rosewall in the most one-sided final in Forest Hills history. The scores were 6-1, 6-0, 6-1.

Virtually his whole life has been wrapped up in tennis. Born in East St. Louis, Illinois, Jimmy grew up in Belleville, Illinois, where he was given his first racquet at the age of 3. His love and ability for the sport came naturally. They were inherited from his mother and grandmother, both of whom had been players, and they were his first tutors.

When he was 15, the family moved to Los Angeles so that Jimmy could be coached by Pancho Segura, a former high-ranking professional and one of the most astute analysts of the game. Success arrived rapidly for Jimmy. He won several national junior titles. His first important victory as a senior was the National Intercollegiate championship in 1971 when he was a student at the University of California at Los Angeles. Since then he has been the winner of many major tournaments in the United States and also in other countries.

A left-hander on his forehand, Jimmy switches to a two-handed grip on his backhand. Known as a fiery competitor, he never lets up on the court and never lets a point go by default. In top condition (he tries to run a few miles every day and skip rope), he races about the court, constantly keeping the pressure on his opponent. He is famous for his low sharply angled cross-court drives, hitting the ball on the early rise, and then rushing in for the finishing volley.

Jimmy Connors (left) holds aloft the trophy he earned by winning the United States Open tennis championship at Forest Hills. Ken Rosewall of Australia, who lost to Connors in the final round, is sitting in the foreground. Connors (below) reaches out to make a forehand return during his match with Rosewall.
UPI photos

Always in motion, Jimmy Connors displays the form that made him the No. 1-ranking player in the United States. In top photo he stretches for a forehand return; in above photo he prepares to wallop the ball with his two-fisted backhand, and in photo at right he moves in for a forehand volley.
UPI photos

FOREWORD

The neighborhood in which I grew up recognized only three sports—football, basketball, and baseball. As the seasons changed, we played football on the empty grassy lots between houses, and the other two sports at the local school playground. My earliest impression of tennis was that it was an activity indulged in by social dandies wearing white flannel trousers who didn't seem to sweat very much and didn't take winning or losing very seriously.

That started to change upon my graduation from junior high school when an aunt presented me with an inexpensive tennis racquet strung with silk (yes, that's how long ago it was). My first expedition to a run-down clay court with a friend was a disaster. The balls we hit almost invariably boomed into the wire fence or plopped into the net. To serve and play a regular set was out of the question.

However, in time and with much practice, I improved. By the end of my high-school years, I had left organized team sports behind. I now knew the satisfaction of waiting eagerly for a serve, driving it deep to my opponent's backhand, and rushing to the net to put away his weak return. Or setting myself for a down-the-line backhand that would blaze past my foe at the net, who would be lunging futilely for the ball.

As a spectator, during those years, I remember sitting high up in the concrete-horseshoe stadium at Forest Hills, watching my first United States championship final, while Don McNeil outbattled Bobby Riggs in a five-set thriller.

The next year I saw the touring pros in action for the first time at a local college gym. A marvelous doubleheader: Fred Perry vs. Frankie Kovacs and J. Donald Budge vs. Bobby Riggs.

Perry, performing graceful steps along the baseline, engaged in a duel

Charles Lundgren, tennis coach at Upsala College in East Orange, N. J., has been rated one of the finest teaching professionals in the United States. Camp Racquet, his summer training camp at Blair Academy in Blairstown, N. J., is the second oldest in the country. A frequent writer for tennis publications, he is also an officer of many tennis associations and organizations.

of ground strokes with Kovacs (who, the experts said, had more natural talent than anyone in the sport). And Budge, of the fierce serve, overhead and backhand, ultimately conquered a combative Riggs, who made one impossible retrieve after another.

By now the misconceptions of my early youth about tennis had dissolved. It was not a game for sissies. It required skill, grit, stamina, a love of competition—and brains. It was one person against another, who were equals when they faced each other on the court—and the victory did not always belong to the stronger or the swifter, but to the one who employed his rac-quet better, who used superior tactics, and who disguised his deficiencies more cleverly.

As the years tumbled by, tennis continued to be a fascinating and demanding sport for me. The foot slows and the energy flags, but wiser attributes of head and arm make up for the lessening physical powers. In truth, tennis is a sport for all ages and all seasons. And for those who are about to learn this exciting and satisfying sport, I feel a sense of pleasure. I am certain you will find tennis greatly rewarding and that it will enrich your life as it has mine.

Lud Duroska

Lud Duroska, of The New York Times sports staff, has been interested in tennis for many years. He was a finalist for two successive years in the Irvington (N. J.) juniors' tournament, though he never did earn a varsity letter in school. Before joining The New York Times, Mr. Duroska covered all the major tennis events in the East for the Newark Star-Ledger, including the Nationals at Forest Hills and the Davis Cup Challenge Rounds.

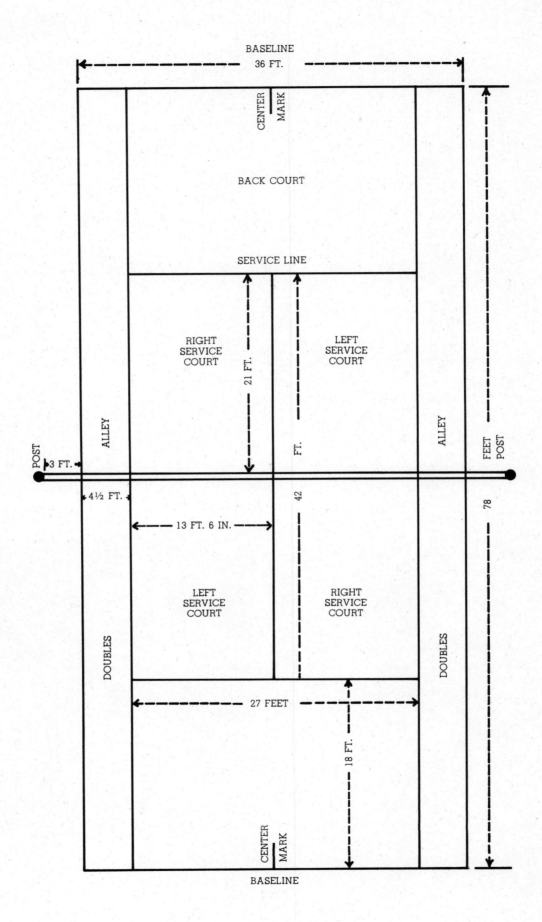

"TENNIS, ANYONE?"

History

If a British cavalry officer by the name of Major Walter C. Wingfield had had his way, the expression on the courts today would be "Sphairistike, anyone?" That difficult-to-pronounce word (which is Greek and means "play ball") was the name he had chosen for the sport.

Although there is some controversy about it, Major Wingfield is generally considered to be the inventor of the sport of lawn tennis, which is now more commonly called tennis. Why he selected such an exotic, foreign word as sphairistike for his invention has never been established by the historians.

What is known is that Major Wingfield, in 1874, obtained a patent on his game after having a pamphlet printed that gave the rules, some advice on how to play the game, and a diagram of the court, which was shaped in the form of an hourglass. Although he was a descendant of an illustrious and once well-to-do British family, the Major's financial situation was somewhat precarious, so he was interested in earning money by selling the equipment —the racquets, the balls, the posts, the netting and other materials—necessary to build a court and participate in the sport.

Unfortunately for him, the Major never did realize any significant monetary returns. One reason was that critics claimed he had merely combined elements of court tennis and badminton, which had been played for years, and they refused to buy his pamphlet or his equipment. Another reason was that others interested in the sport almost immediately began to revise the rules and change the shape and dimensions of the court, thereby making the Major's version obsolete.

By 1875 the All-England Croquet Club in Wimbledon, a suburb of London, added several grass courts to its grounds and included "lawn tennis" in its name, hoping to gain more members. The new sport proved to be an attraction and was so popular with the club membership that croquet was pushed into the background in the next few years.

The club held its first Wimbledon championship in June, 1877, on courts that were now rectangular and measured 78 feet long and 27 feet wide. Almost unbelievably, those dimensions have remained the same to this day. The net for that first Wimbledon tournament was 3 feet 3 inches high at the center and the posts supporting the net at each end were 5 feet high. For some time those heights varied until they were standardized at 3 feet at the center of the net and 3 feet 6 inches for the posts.

Miss Mary Outerbridge is credited with introducing the sport in America in 1874, having learned about the game while on vacation in Bermuda, where she had watched British officers playing it. She brought back a net, racquets and balls. With the help of her brother, A. Emilius Outerbridge, she marked out the first court (which was hourglass-shaped) on the grounds of the Staten Island Cricket and Baseball Club.

The sport quickly spread to other private clubs throughout New England and the Middle Atlantic states, but with variations in rules, the size of the ball, the height of the net, and the scoring. After the first important tournament was staged in Staten Island in 1880, the prominent players, particularly two brothers, Dr. Dwight and Richard Sears, recognized the need for making all aspects of the game uniform. The next year representatives of more than 20 clubs met in New York and organized the United States Lawn Tennis Association, which has continued to be the major governing body of the sport in America to the present time.

Even if little has remained of Major

Wingfield's original concept, it seems only fair that he should be given credit for providing the idea and the impetus for one of the few truly international sports, a sport that is played and followed by millions in virtually every country in the world.

Racquets

Since the inception of the sport, all racquets were made of wood until several years ago when the steel racquet appeared and then the aluminum racquet. Both gained a measure of popularity, especially among the leading players to whom the higher prices of the metal racquets are not a factor.

Wood, however, remains a favorite. The most important reason for this preference is that wood allows you to "feel" a shot, because it absorbs the vibrations and thus aids tremendously in

The three types of racquets that are in general use today.

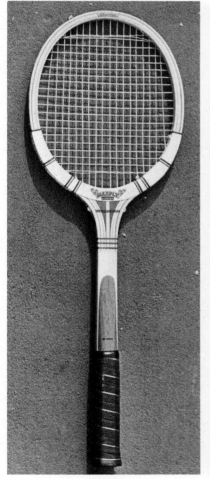

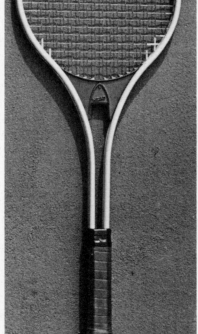

Wood   **Steel**   **Aluminum**

your shot-making. The disadvantage of wood is that the frame tends to warp if the racquet gets wet (a waterproof cover is naturally recommended) or after many restringing jobs.

The steel racquet tends to provide more power. With its streamlined, open-throat construction, it encounters less air resistance and tends to flex and unflex in a trampoline-like action. This advantage is most noticeable when serving, but steel also tends to make ground strokes harder to control. Some players have found that steel has too much flexibility for their liking and so they have returned to using wood, giving up the strength of steel for the better "feel" of wood.

The aluminum racquet, which has become quite popular recently, is light and strong. It possesses some flexibility, but not as much as steel, and it also has some of the "cushioned" feel of wood. Thus, aluminum's features represent a kind of modification of the other two.

For the beginner, the wood racquet would be the best choice until he or she is experienced enough to experiment with the metal racquets.

In the choice of racquet stringing, the learner is advised to select nylon over gut. Important considerations are that nylon costs about half the price of gut and is more durable. Since nylon is more resistant to moisture, you will be able to play on wet days or when the balls are damp. Gut offers greater power and resiliency, but will stretch if it gets damp. After you have developed your game, you should switch to

gut stringing, because you will then be able to use it more advantageously.

Selecting a racquet of the proper weight is essential. A racquet that is too light will be easy to swing but will reduce the power of your shotmaking. A racquet that is too heavy will slow your swing and impair your timing.

Racquets come in three weights—light, medium and heavy. For a player in his or her early teens, a light racquet of 12 to 13 ounces is likely to be best. For older teen-agers, a medium weight of 13 to 14½ ounces would appear to be desirable. Any racquet weighing about 15 ounces is considered heavy and should be left for the strongest and most experienced players.

Handle size is also important. Generally, for a girl, a handle 4½ inches in circumference should suffice. For a boy, 4⅝ inches is the average. Only if you have a big hand should you consider a larger handle.

It is also well to check the balance of your racquet, which is 27 inches long. The midpoint should be 13½ inches from the handle. If there is a variation in the balance, it is better to have the racquet heavier in the handle. If the balance point is toward the head, the racquet probably will prove too unwieldly.

Clothing

Until recent years, players were required to wear white clothes. It was the only color permitted to be worn in tournaments and at clubs. But that situa-

Andrea Bobby (left) and Tom Mullen are fashionably dressed for an afternoon of tennis.

tion has changed and more colorful garb is now acceptable everywhere. Your tennis garments should allow you complete freedom of movement but not be so loose as to get in your way. If the clothes are too tight, they will hamper your pursuit and hitting of the ball.

Boys invariably wear shorts or short-shorts, sometimes with a stripe or v-cut on the sides. Soft blue or yellow pastels are popular colors, besides the traditional white. The shirt is customarily short-sleeved and the collar-type is often favored. The standard tennis socks are generally white, although many prefer those with red, white and blue piping or stripes. Canvas-type sneakers are worn by most players, but the soft-leather type, which has come into style, is also popular.

Girls are usually similarly attired in shorts and sleeveless shirts with collars. Some prefer the stylish tennis dresses, which are made attractively in several colors.

The wearing of a tennis cap or hat is a matter of personal preference. Most players don't wear either one, but a cap can be useful on a very sunny day in the summer. Also, some players wear a cap in the fall when the sun is low in the sky and they are facing into the sun.

It is a good idea to have a tennis sweater or jacket handy to keep warm. When you have completed a match and are perspiring, it is wise to put on a jacket to keep the muscles warm while you cool off gradually.

Scoring

The quaint scoring terminology in tennis has probably discouraged, at least for a while, more than one person from taking up the sport. But actually it is not as complicated as it may sound at first.

"Love" is the word for zero, and the first four points, instead of being called 1, 2, 3 and 4, are 15, 30, 40 and game. However, a game has to be won by at least a two-point margin. So, if the score is 40-40, that is called deuce. If the server wins the next point, it is called his advantage or advantage in. If he then wins the next point, he takes the game. If his opponent wins the first point after deuce, it is called his advantage (also ad) or advantage out. If the server loses the next point after

gaining the advantage point, the score reverts back to deuce.

So that you can easily tell who is leading in a game, the server's score is always given first. For example, if he has won the first two points, the score is 30-love. If his opponent then takes the next three points, the score is 30-40.

To win a set, you must win at least six games with a two-game margin. This naturally leads to many long sets, with such scores as 8-6, 11-9, 13-11, and so on. Partly because of the demands of television, but mostly to sustain crowd interest by avoiding lengthy matches, the nine-point tie-breaker was invented. When a set reaches 6-6, the player who would normally serve the 13th game (the service until then has alternated each game between the players), serves the first, second, fifth and sixth points, and his opponent the third, fourth, seventh, eighth and ninth points. Of course, the tie-breaker is over as soon as one player wins five points. The set score then reads 7-6.

The players change sides on the odd games, starting after the first game. In the tie-breaker, the players change sides after the fourth point.

Matches are either two-of-three sets or three-of-five sets. The latter is considered the championship distance and is the required format in major national and international competitions, including the Davis Cup. The set scores are given with the winner's first so that if the winner has lost the first and third sets, the scores could read: 4-6, 6-2, 3-6, 7-6, 6-4.

GRIPS

The proper grip is the first step in learning how to play tennis. The grips that are recommended are the Eastern forehand-drive grip, the Eastern backhand-drive grip, and the Continental serve grip, which is also used for all other strokes except the drive. These grips also happen to be the onès most popular with the majority of today's better players.

Before describing how to position your hand and fingers for each grip, it is important that you remember to hold the racquet firmly but not so tightly that you lose flexibility in making your stroke. Don't go to the other extreme and hold the racquet too loosely. You will know if you are doing that because the racquet will turn in your hand at the moment of impact with the ball.

Now on to the correct way of gripping the racquet:

For the forehand-drive grip, hold the throat of the racquet with your non-playing hand. The face of the racquet should be perpendicular to the ground and the handle should be horizontal. Reach out and shake hands with the handle, making certain the palm is on the back of the handle and perpendic-

Forehand Drive side view

ular to the ground. Most important, the hand should be cupped naturally around the handle in a "shake-hands" grip (left photo), with the junction between the thumb and the index finger on top of the handle.

The right photo shows the proper grip as seen from the back. Notice that the index finger is slightly advanced and separated.

For the backhand-drive grip, the palm of the hand is brought on top of the racquet. The thumb is diagonally across the back and the junction be-

Forehand Drive back view

tween the index finger and thumb is on the little beveled edge on the left topside of the racquet (left photo). The fingers are spread, the face of the racquet is again perpendicular, and the handle is again horizontal. In short, the hand is turned on top of the racquet.

From the back view, the main feature of the proper grip (right photo) is that the index finger is well advanced up the handle of the racquet.

For the serve grip (called the Continental grip), the palm of the hand is flat against the beveled edge of the

Backhand Drive side view

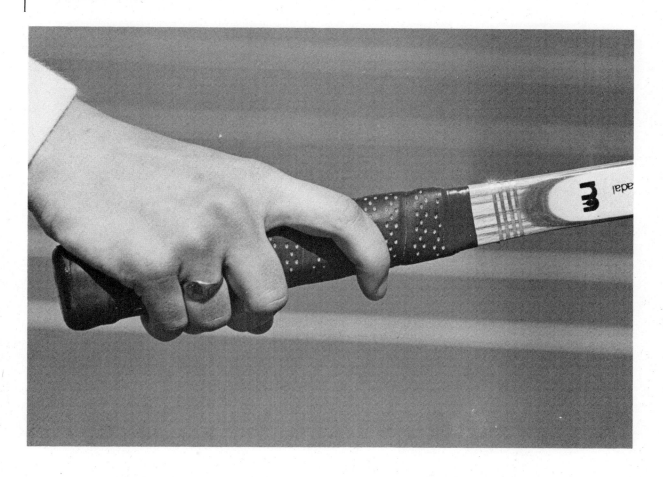

right topside of the racquet. The junction between the thumb and the index finger is on the left top crease, and the index finger is spread (left photo).

Looking from the front side (right photo), notice that the thumb is hooked around the racquet and the heel of the hand is on top.

A grip seldom used now is the Western forehand grip, which was developed years ago on the West Coast. Interestingly, the recommended grips also received their names because of the geographical area in which they

Serve (Continental) side view

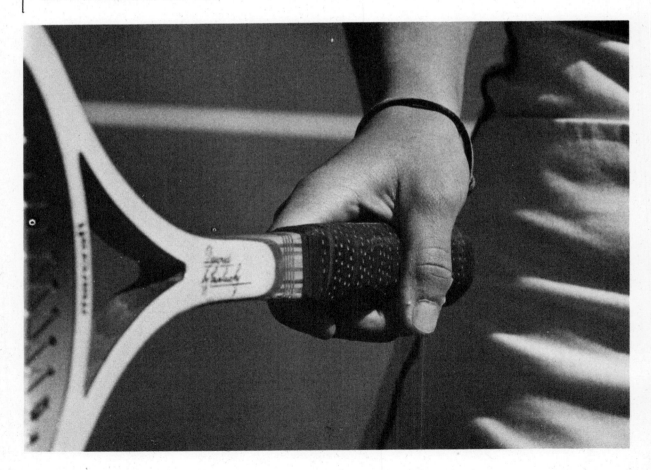

Serve (Continental) back view

were developed—the Eastern for the eastern part of the United States and the Continental for the continent of Europe, referring to France in particular.

For the Western grip (left photo), the face of the racquet should be perpendicular. Take hold of the racquet with your palm underneath and thumb across the top.

From the back view (right photo), it will be seen that the fingers are more compressed than in the Eastern forehand grip.

Billy Johnston, a star in the 1910's

Western side view

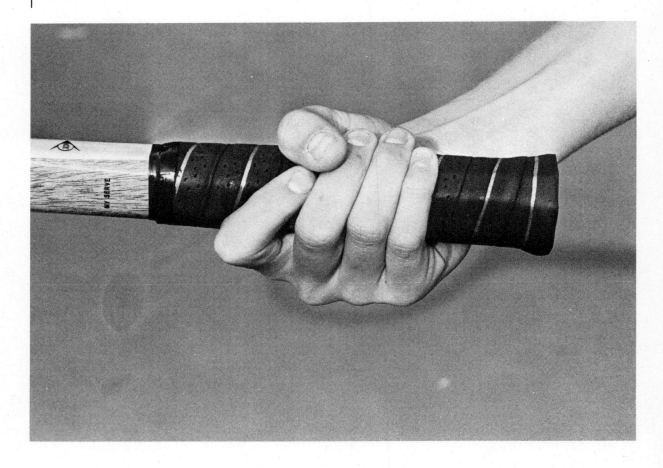

and 1920's who frequently met Bill Tilden in the finals of many important tournaments, was probably the most famous player to use the Western grip. The grip helps to impart topspin, especially on balls that bounce high on a fast surface, such as concrete, which was a common surface in the West. However, the grip puts a great deal of pressure on the elbow and such strokes are difficult to control, especially on low balls, and for these reasons the grip has been discarded by most players. The grip is definitely not recommended for beginners or intermediate players.

Western back view

FOREHAND

This stroke provides the foundation on which to build a sound game. You will hit more shots with your forehand than with any other stroke.

To get into the ready position, face the net with your feet shoulder-width apart. Flex your knees and bend forward at the waist. Place the left hand on the throat of the racquet (for guidance and to reduce strain on the racquet hand). Keep your weight forward on the balls of your feet.

As the ball approaches, pivot your body and turn the right foot so that it is parallel to the baseline. Draw the racquet back so that it is lower than the ball to be hit, step forward (toward the net) with your left foot, and allow your weight to shift to that foot as you hit the ball. Your eyes should never leave the ball until you actually hit it. Swing the racquet forward and upward, keeping the wrist still and the grip firm, and allow the body to pivot. Continue the swing until the racquet has traveled around your body, ending on your left with its opposite face turned somewhat toward your opponent's court.

The follow-through controls the forehand drive. If you don't hit through the ball, it may go sailing in any direction. Don't be afraid to follow through. You should complete the arc of your swing, even on the slowest and easiest shots. Indecision will ruin the shot. Make up your mind, then swing decisively.

As you practice the forehand, you will find that the best results come from a continuous, unbroken motion. A consistent rhythm is important; a hitch anywhere along the line reduces effectiveness.

Try to hit every shot at the level of your waist, moving in or back to do so. If the ball should bounce so low that it never rises to your waist, bend the knees and bring your waist down to the ball. Don't stand up straight and try to shovel a low shot. It's just not good that way.

The forehand is the key to the backcourt game and is equally important in attacking or defending. It can be used to win points outright by means of blasting speed or crafty placement, and it can also be used to return the ball when you wish to outsteady your opponent (wait for him to make the error). That's why it's best to learn this shot first and to try to make it as sound as possible.

One warning: if you start your backswing too late, the racquet will go around in a hurried loop. The result will be an erratic and uncontrolled shot, which is not good. You must take your racquet back the moment you realize that the ball is coming to your forehand. Be alert and attentive without feeling strained.

By practicing constantly, both by yourself (against a wall) or with an opponent on the other side of the net, you will find, one day, that you are hitting the forehand with automatic motions. It's known as "grooving" your shot. Once you achieve this stage, you should be able to hit a good forehand from anywhere on the court and in almost any position. It's what all good players strive for.

Which players have the best forehands today? Bjorn Borg of Sweden, though only a teen-ager, is probably number one. Manuel Santana of Spain was rated as having the best forehand before he went into retirement a few years ago. Stan Smith also rates high, along with Tom Okker of the Netherlands.

If we go back many years, the names that stand out are Bill Tilden, Ellsworth Vines, Jack Kramer, and Fred Perry. Borg and Okker differ from all these forehand artists in that they use an excessive amount of spin on their shots, as opposed to hitting them flatly.

1. In the waiting position, Tom keeps his feet separated, not close together. His waist and knees are bent and relaxed so that he can move easily. Cupping the throat of the racquet with his left hand and keeping it away from his body, he can move the racquet more quickly than he could with just one hand holding the handle.

2. As Tom takes the backswing, his racquet should point to the back fence. He stands with his side to the net in a baseball hitter's stance. One foot is in front of the other, fanned slightly toward the net, so that when he leans in, his knee will bend forward. His elbow is slightly bent and relaxed so he can get a spanking motion as well as a swinging motion from the shoulder.

3. As the ball approaches, Tom brings his racquet forward. His elbow begins to straighten out, his wrist is firm, and he starts to pivot and lean in, transferring his weight to his front foot.

4. Tom is about to hit the ball; his racquet is almost parallel to the ground and his arm is extended. He has shifted more weight to his front leg.

5. Impact has been made. Tom's racquet follows the path of the ball with a long follow-through. His arm is extended and his wrist is still firm. His weight has been transferred to the front foot, indicated by the raised right heel and the turned body.

6. For the follow-through, Tom has reached out as far as he comfortably can. The pivot of his body and the transfer of his weight is complete as he faces the net.

1.

4.

2.

3.

5.

6.

Forehand   27

1. From the front view, Andrea is in the ready position, her feet well spread and her waist and knees bent as she watches the ball intently.

2. At the beginning of the backswing, she turns her back, or right, foot so that it is parallel to the baseline. She stands with her side almost to the net and brings her racquet back.

3. Completing the backswing, she has placed her weight on the back leg. She starts to pivot, with her left hand forward.

4. Her eyes still on the ball, Andrea begins to shift her weight as she brings her racquet forward.

5. The ball has already left her racquet and she watches its flight; the balance has been shifted to the front foot.

6. On the follow-through, her racquet reaches toward the net and her arm is properly extended to full length.

7. Ending the stroke, Andrea completes the follow-through with the toes of her back, or left, foot pointing to the ground like a ballet dancer's.

1.

4.

5.

2.

3.

6.

7.

Faults in Form

1. With his left foot turned in and his toes together, Tom cannot move quickly in any direction. His feet should be slightly fanned out, as though he were skating, so that he can shift to either side and still retain his balance.

2. His backswing is overextended: too far out and too high. Because most balls come in waist-high or lower, he will have to loop under to hit the ball or hit with a cutting motion.

3. He is off balance. Instead of transferring his weight forward as he swings, he leaves his weight on the back foot. The tendency will be to strike the ball up in the air and too long.

4. He completes a forehand drive. Instead of reaching out and catching the throat of the racquet in his left hand, he drops his hand to the ground, which means he cannot snap the racquet back into position quickly.

5. Andrea's main fault is that her wrist is dropping, causing the racquet to point to the ground. Also, her body is much too straight; it should be bent from the waist. Her feet, parallel to the baseline, should be fanned like an ice skater's.

6. Instead of swinging through and out, she has brought her arm in so that she appears to be hugging herself. She is unable to make a natural flowing stroke, especially with her elbow pulled in.

7. She pulls the racquet into her stomach, producing a cramped position. Also, her left arm hangs down awkwardly.

8. She is off balance on this forehand drive because she has not shifted her weight at all to her front foot.

1. 2. 3. 4.

5. 6. 7. 8.

PRACTICE · HINTS · REMINDERS

Practice

Practice only the forehand drive and work on it for at least twenty minutes each day.

Strive for proper form.

Hit slowly until you master the stroke.

Strive for consistency and accuracy.

As you improve, practice hitting from corner to corner; first cross-court drives, then down-the-line shots.

Get a steady opponent or use the ball-hitting machine. If necessary, have someone toss balls to you.

Practice against a wall is an excellent way to learn.

Hints

Don't hit hard while learning because it inhibits development of proper form.

Try to position yourself as perfectly as possible each time by moving your feet.

See the impact.

Reminders

Relax between shots.

Keep your eye on the ball.

BACKHAND

Most beginners are afraid of the backhand. This is a paradox because the backhand is a more natural stroke than the forehand. In the forehand the player must hit around the body; in the backhand the body does not interfere with the smooth movement of the stroke. So get rid of any bugaboo you have about the backhand. Once you do so, the battle is half-won.

In learning the forehand, you also learn much about the backhand: the ready position and the pattern of the motion of the swing.

Most players have more strength on their forehand side, but the naturalness of the backhand should compensate for that. Like the forehand, it should be hit in one continuous motion. The ingredients are: an early, shorter swing straight back, with no frills (such as loops, which some players like to use on the forehand for the sake of rhythm and timing); a closed stance with shoulders perpendicular to the net; cradling the racquet comfortably in the left hand; a free, easy swing through the ball with the arm fully extended at moment of impact. The racquet should be imagined as an extension of your arm. Never crowd the ball; use the full length of your racquet and arm together. And don't forget to follow through.

Again, with your eyes on the ball, pivot and turn the left foot so it is parallel to baseline, and step forward with your right foot, allowing your weight to shift to that foot, and meet the ball. Forget about poking or jabbing at the ball, or lashing at it hurriedly. Swing! The ball must be taken well in front and waist high to produce an effective shot.

Like the forehand, the backhand is used to return the serve (both for attacking and defending); to make passing shots against a net player; to make approach shots in going to the net; to hit a clean winner; to open the opponent's court and maneuver him out of position and so open the opponent's court; and to get out of trouble when forced into a bad position.

How hard should you hit the ball?

Most of the time it's done with average pace, only occasionally with full power.

Why do some players look so awkward while making this shot? In most cases it's because the elbow is leading the arm. The problem could begin in the backswing, for instead of taking the arm back with the elbow close to the body and at waist level, the player allows the elbow to protrude. It loses all contact with the body and is at a much higher level than the waist. Sometimes the player uses only his forearm and so punches from the elbow instead of swinging and pivoting the body, instead of his shoulder and body.

One solution is to keep the elbow tucked against the body in the backswing and to hit the ball with a straight arm until the old pattern is forgotten.

What about the use of the wrist? That depends on the individual player. There are great backhands with almost no wrist action, and there are equally great backhands in which the wrist movement is the prominent feature. Only those with natural talent can get away with wrist-flicking in the backhand. Remember that flicking the wrist requires split-second timing, but it gives more power and can disguise the shot better. However, a more sound backhand can be developed if the wrist action is minimized.

Among players having outstanding backhands, two names stand out: Ken Rosewall, of Australia, among today's players, and Don Budge, among the former greats.

1. Watching for the oncoming ball, Tom is again relaxed at the waist and knees, in the ready position. He cups the throat of the racquet with his left hand as he waits to see which side the ball will land on.

2. He now turns to begin the backswing. The back, or left, foot will be parallel to the baseline when he ends the backswing with his racquet drawn back.

3. The backswing completed, his racquet points to the back fence. He is just beginning to shift his weight forward.

4. As Tom brings his racquet forward, he shifts the balance of his weight from his back leg to his front leg. Note that his eyework is perfect. He watches the ball so closely that he could probably read the brand name on the ball if he had to.

5. He has made contact with the ball and has followed the flight of the ball with his racquet on the follow-through.

6. He now points his fully extended arm toward the net. He has shifted his weight completely to the front foot.

7. Tom has ended the follow-through and pivoted so that the racquet points to the right corner of the court.

1.

4.

5.

2.

3.

6.

7.

1. In the waiting position, Andrea's body is properly bent and she is ready to turn rapidly to either her forehand or backhand side.

2. She sees that the ball has been hit to her backhand, so she picks up her left foot and starts out in pursuit of the ball.

3. She holds the racquet with both hands, keeping its face slightly open. With her arm wrapped around her body like a banner, she will plant her left foot and start her swing.

4. As she puts her front foot down, she leans in and shifts her balance forward as she swings.

5. Andrea makes contact with the ball with a firm wrist, her weight shifting to her front foot.

6. Her racquet drives through the ball as she continues to pivot, and she keeps her eyes on the ball.

7. Completing the follow-through, she ends in the proper position, facing the net.

1.

4.

5.

2.

3.

6.

7.

Faults in Form

1. Tom falls away from the ball as he attempts to hit a backhand from a cramped position and loses his balance. He should be positioned much farther away from the ball so that he can hit it with a properly extended arm.

2. A common fault on the backhand drive is to flick the wrist and snap around. Andrea should swing with her whole arm.

3. She falls back as she swings, unable to transfer her weight from her back leg to her front leg, as correct form requires.

PRACTICE · HINTS · REMINDERS

Practice

Practice only the backhand drive for at least twenty minutes each day.

Keep the emphasis on form, steadiness, and accuracy.

Keep your speed down; it is your enemy in the beginning.

As you progress, design cross-court drills. Later, do down-the-line drills.

Hints

Watch the ball. See the impact.

Position yourself properly.

Reminder

Relax between shots.

SERVE

The serve is one of the most important strokes in the game. If you serve well, you put your opponent at a disadvantage at the very start. Try to develop a dependable serve that will go in the court most of the time. You are allowed two serves on every point. If you miss with the first, be sure to get the second in, since a double-fault will not only cost you a point, but will also shake your confidence.

The serving motion should be something like a chain reaction in which the body and shoulders move into the ball, the elbow extends, and the wrist snaps through at impact. The power derives from the coordinated speed of the action. It is a more complicated stroke than either the forehand or backhand, since both hands must be coordinated and the right arm and body have a more difficult task to perform.

The motion of the arm on the serve is almost like a baseball throw. To stand in the correct position, place the left foot just behind the baseline at a 45-degree angle to it, and the right foot a comfortable distance behind the left and parallel to the baseline. The ball should be tossed at least as high as you can extend the racquet over your head. You should be consistent with the toss, otherwise you cannot gain accuracy.

The goal is to coordinate the toss with the swing. You must guide yourself through the swing. The left hand, which holds the balls, should be on the face of the racquet or the shaft. Start both hands downward together. When they arrive at waist level, they should part, the left making the toss, the right going back in the throwing motion. At this point, your back should be arched to gain power and momentum. You swing forward, shifting weight from the right to the left foot. The right arm now is fully extended, and it should make contact with the ball at its zenith and out in front. Keep your head up, looking at the ball until you make contact—that's essential if you want to meet the ball squarely. It also helps to avoid bringing your shoulder down, which might result in hitting the ball into the net.

Finish the stroke with a snap of the wrist and let the racquet fall on the left side. The body has come around and the back foot has swung into the court. With the follow-through completed, move quickly to the ready position at the baseline, or if you have learned to volley well, move in to the net.

The serve is one shot you can work on by yourself after learning the technique. Get a basket of balls, go out to the court, and serve at targets set up in the opposite service boxes. Try a hard, flat serve, then a spin second serve. Don't try to hit the ball with all your power. Only top players can get away with that, because if they miss with their first serve, they also have a good second serve. But the beginner

cannot afford to do that. He must try to serve with controlled speed.

Rhythm and momentum are the keys to good serving. There can be no jerking or gyration in the execution. The three different kinds of serves you should learn—flat, spin, and slice—are basically hit the same way, with small differences in the toss and the forward part of the swing.

In a recent test, Colin Dibley of Australia was credited with having the fastest serve in tennis today at 147 miles an hour. The serve was measured not only for speed but also for consistency. Dibley beat out such tremendously fast servers as Arthur Ashe, Roscoe Tanner, John Alexander, and John Newcombe.

Despite his overpowering serve, though, Dibley is not considered a high-ranking world player because the rest of his game is weak.

Still rated among the best servers is Pancho Gonzales. Unlike most of today's players, Gonzales does not use an exaggerated windup in serving. His motion is easy and economical, and the secret of his success is that the delivery is made with a controlled rhythm that "explodes" at the moment of contact.

As for the great servers of the past, Bill Tilden, Don Budge, Ellsworth Vines, and Jack Kramer head the list. They could hit the flat or cannonball serve with enormous speed and power. If the first serve missed the box, they resorted to the twist, putting spin on the ball so that it "kicked" sharply away from the receiver.

1. Getting ready to serve, Tom looks toward the area where he is going to serve the ball.

2. He tosses the ball up and starts his backswing.

3. With the racquet behind his back, forming a right angle between forearm and handle, he leans toward the net. His back is arched as he prepares to spring forward.

4. Having dropped his racquet, he is ready to snap his arm up and over the top and at the same time let his body fall into the court.

5. Tom is shown at full stretch, reaching out with his arm completely extended to meet the ball.

6. With the racquet following the flight of the ball, he puts all of his weight behind his swing for the serve and delivers the correct follow-through. The player must allow the racquet to fall into a natural position rather than try to apply brakes.

7. At the end of the serve, the racquet has crossed over the body in a motion similar to that of a baseball pitcher after he has thrown the ball.

1.

4.

5.

2.

3.

6.

7.

1. Andrea prepares to serve as she brings the racquet up to waist level and touches it with the ball, a common habit among players.

2. In the same rhythmic motion she tosses the ball up with her left hand and extends her racquet straight up.

3. With the ball at the peak of the toss (ball not in photo), she has completed the backswing. Her left arm is thrust out to help maintain body balance, and she keeps her eyes on the ball.

4. About to hit the ball, Andrea displays good form in reaching as high as she can with her racquet and also rising on her toes in order to make maximum use of her height.

5. She has sent the serve on its way, putting her body and arm into the stroke, and she has pivoted toward the net.

6. Her momentum is carrying her forward into the court in the midst of her follow-through.

7. With the racquet now crossing her body and ending on her left side, she finishes the follow-through.

1.

4.

5.

2.

3.

6.

7.

Faults in Form

1. Andrea stands in an awkward position, with the racquet too low and her arm too close to her body. She has tossed up the ball, but her arm has already dropped. She should be reaching back, her body arched and ready to hit the ball.

2. A poor ready position. The racquet is held too high above the waist, and her weight is on the front foot.

3. With the ball just starting to drop, she is leaning in much too early and is almost falling into the court.

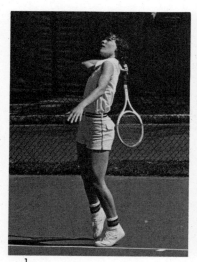

1.

2.

3.

PRACTICE · HINTS · REMINDERS

Practice

Spend twenty minutes practicing only the serve.

Strive for correct form, steadiness and accuracy.

As you progress, serve at targets (a racquet cover, a piece of cardboard, or other object) placed in the corners of the service boxes.

Hints

See the impact.

Don't look away as you start a forward swing.

Make sure you align your feet and body properly (see text).

Reminder

Fling your arm and racquet at the ball; don't push, or strain on the fore-swing.

APPROACH SHOT

When your opponent makes a weak return and hits a short ball to the mid-court area, particularly inside the service line, you have the opportunity to execute the approach shot. This stroke is meant to begin the attack on your opponent. You run forward toward the ball, and after completing the approach shot, you are in position to proceed to the fore-court and prepare for the volley.

The approach shot should be hit forcefully and deep so that the return, if it comes at all, will be easy to handle and will enable you either to volley or smash the ball away.

The approach shot is somewhat similar to a volley in that the backswing is short and the ball is punched. However, the follow-through is longer than that of the volley.

Beginners should not try to hit approach shots for winners. The emphasis, rather, should be on hitting deep and making down-the-line shots on either the forehand or the backhand side. Approach shots are meant to allow you to get into the volley position at the net.

The approach shot is usually not hit cross-court but down the line because it gives your opponent less time to react and also reduces the chances of an angled return.

Forehand

1. Andrea moves forward to hit the ball shortly after it bounces. She will use a short backswing somewhat similar to that used for a volley.

2. With her backswing slightly down, she sets herself for the punching stroke. For the moment, her weight is on her back foot.

1.

2.

3. Andrea brings her racquet forward as she watches the ball intently.

4. As she hits the ball, her weight has shifted forward to her front foot.

5. She is in the midst of her follow-through, pivoting toward the net.

6. She completes the follow-through and now will move into a volleying position closer to the net.

———————

7. When Tom moves into midcourt to take a short ball on the run, he starts a short backswing.

8. Having punched the ball with an abbreviated swing, he has already shifted his weight to the front foot. He continues to watch the ball.

9. His follow-through is slightly longer than it should be as he finishes the stroke.

3.

6.

7.

4.

5.

8.

9.

Approach Shot   51

PRACTICE · HINTS · REMINDERS

Practice

Have a friend hit a series of short balls to you so they bounce in the service box on your forehand side. Run from the baseline to the ball and practice your forehand approach shot.

Go back to the baseline and repeat the procedure.

Practice for at least twenty minutes each time.

Hints

Keep your backswing short.

Punch the ball with a short forward motion.

Reminder

Hit with pace, but don't overhit. Be sure the ball goes deep.

Backhand

1. Preparing for a backhand approach shot, Andrea is about to transfer her weight from the back foot after a short backswing.

2. As she leans in and makes contact with the ball, her body balance has definitely shifted to the front foot.

3. She punches the ball, meeting it well in front of her body, and keeps her eyes on the ball.

1.

2.

3.

4. As the ball leaves her racquet, Andrea begins her follow-through.

5. She is well forward as she ends the follow-through.

———

6. Seeing that his opponent's return will be short, Tom moves quickly into mid-court.

7. Taking a short backswing, he is now in position to make his backhand approach shot.

8. He shows great concentration as he completes the backswing. His feet are placed so he can lean into the ball.

9. His body balance has shifted forward as he leans into the ball and takes a nice, vigorous punch.

10. He ends the stroke with the proper follow-through.

4.

7.

8.

5.

6.

9.

10.

PRACTICE · HINTS · REMINDERS

Practice

Follow the practice tips given for the forehand approach shot.

Hint

Be sure to twist your body sideways so you can get some pivot into the backhand approach shot.

Reminders

Keep the backswing short.

Focus your eyes on the ball.

VOLLEY

When a player goes on the attack, the objective is to get to the net, from where he can hit a volley (taking the ball on the fly) for a placement.

The correct volleying area is about 6 to 10 feet from the net. It becomes more difficult to volley when you are farther back. Be sure that your racquet is higher than your wrist at the moment of impact. When the ball is hit to you above the level of the net, it is possible to go for a winning placement. A volley should be punched and aimed well away from your opponent, either hit deep with force or hit more gently at a sharp cross-court angle.

Many beginners forget to bend their knees when they attempt to hit a low shot, which will frequently result in netting the ball. Try to get as low as you can on these shots to avert the error.

After the volley, step toward the net in the direction of your hit. Many players tend to move to the center of the forecourt, thinking it's the best place to cover the net, but it is not. Move forward to the side of the court to which you have made your shot so that your opponent will find it difficult to attempt a passing shot down the sideline. Even though you leave room at the other side, the chances of your opponent hitting a successful cross-court passing shot are very slim.

One final note. Volleying is often mistakenly used to describe an exchange of shots. The correct word for that is "rally."

Forehand

1. Looking at the ball, Tom is ready to volley. His body is bent at the waist, his feet are apart, and his elbows are relaxed.

2. He moves to receive the ball by stepping diagonally toward it with his left foot. He shifts his balance forward and turns his side to the net. The backswing is short, and he leans over, ready to punch the ball.

3. With elbow cocked and racquet angled up, Tom is in proper position for the volley.

4. Tom makes impact with the ball with a quick punch. His weight shifts forward.

5. His body is relaxed at the finish. He has shifted his weight from back leg to front leg.

1.

2.

3.

4.

5.

1. In the waiting position, Andrea is bent at the waist, knees relaxed and feet apart, and her racquet is held up.

2. She prepares to move to her right to be in position for a forehand volley.

3. After a short backswing, she steps forward to make the shot.

4. Andrea is making the correct punching action as she concentrates on the area to which she wants to volley the ball.

5. Leaning over and shifting her weight forward, she completes the short follow-through.

1.

4.

5.

2.

3.

Fault in Form

1. Her body is too erect, not bent over. Also, her left arm is dangling.

1.

PRACTICE · HINTS · REMINDERS

Practice

While you are positioned at the net, ask a friend to hit a series of balls to your forehand side so you can practice your forehand volley.

Practice your volley for at least twenty minutes.

At first, be satisfied to volley into the court.

As you progress, volley to targets placed in the far corners of the backcourt.

Practice your short and angled volleys to targets placed in the outer corners of the service box. These volleys should be hit softer.

Hints

Strike the ball well in front with your wrist laid back.

Remember, a volley is punched, not swung.

Reminders

Keep the backswing and the foreswing short.

Keep your eye on the ball. See the impact.

Backhand

1. Tom is already beginning to make his move, turning his body to the left and getting the racquet back with two hands, but keeping the backswing short.

2. He starts to step forward with his right foot so he can get his weight into the punching stroke.

3. Now ready to hit the volley, Tom begins transferring his weight to the front foot.

1.

2.

3.

4. He has made contact and punches the ball for a placement, still watching its flight.

5. Ending the volley, he shows the short follow-through, and his weight is fully on the front foot.

4.

5.

1. In the ready position, Andrea has the racquet well in front of her, and her body is relaxed with her knees bent.

2. She is turned sideways as she leans forward for the volley.

3. Having hit the ball, she finishes the abbreviated follow-through.

1.

2.

3.

PRACTICE · HINTS · REMINDERS

Practice

While positioned at the net, have a friend hit a series of balls to your backhand side so you can practice your backhand volleys.

Follow the procedure prescribed under the forehand volley.

Hint

Be sure to punch the volley, hitting the ball well in front, with the wrist cocked and laid back.

Reminder

Keep the backswing very short.

LOB

The lob is generally thought of as a defensive stroke, although you can hit an offensive lob by using topspin. However, it is a very tricky shot and it is advisable not to attempt it until you have become competent at defensive lobbing.

An appropriate time to use the lob is when your opponent has been rushing the net regularly and you have been having problems passing him. The lob will force him to retreat from the net. Try to hit the lob high, 20 feet or higher, and as deep into his backcourt as you safely dare. A short or low lob is very dangerous because he is likely to smash it away. Mix lobs and drives so that he is not sure what to expect, thereby putting him on the defensive and breaking the rhythm of his game. Successful lobs also will cause him to think twice and hesitate about his net-rushing tactics.

Another excellent time to lob is whenever you are forced into a weak position, such as running across the court into the alley to recover a ball. The lob is a safer shot than a passing shot whenever you are in an unbalanced position. The lob will give you time to get back to center position and in contention again for the point.

Lobbing also slows the pace of the game if the match has been going against you.

Forehand

1. As the ball arrives, Andrea begins to turn sideways as if she is planning to make a passing shot.

2. Drawing her racquet back, she has still disguised her intention to lob. The purpose is to get her opponent off balance so a lob can be more effectively executed.

3. She begins her lob, sweeping the racquet forward and upward.

4. Opening the racquet face as the swing progresses, she attempts to hit the ball over her opponent's head.

5. She completes the high follow-through.

1.

2.

3.

4.

5.

Backhand

1. While Tom starts to move into position, he begins his backswing.

2. Reaching the ball, he is positioned to stroke a lob. He sweeps the racquet forward, then upward, and opens the racquet face as the swing progresses.

3. He finishes the stroke with a high follow-through and snaps back to a ready position.

1.

2.

3.

PRACTICE · HINTS · REMINDERS

Practice

Position a friend opposite you at the net. As he punches a series of balls to your forehand side, practice your forehand lob. Try to get the ball over his head.

Try to lob so the ball lands within ten feet of the baseline.

After about fifteen minutes, practice your backhand lob.

Hints

It is better to lob too high than too low.

Sweep the ball upward; don't swat at it.

Reminder

Watch the ball! You can't hit it well if you don't see it.

SMASH

The smash (also called an overhead) is one of the most devastating strokes in the game and usually the most spectacular to watch. It is similar to the serve, but is a more complicated shot because you do not govern the descent of the ball and you have to move into position, requiring that you coordinate footwork, body, and racquet arm.

The leading players take the ball out of the air without a bounce. Less experienced players often prefer to let the ball bounce, giving them more time to get into the proper position and increasing the chances of putting the ball away accurately. However, it is better not to let the ball bounce unless it is falling straight down and not at an angle. If the ball bounces at an angle, it will force you to retreat several more steps and make it harder to hit an effective smash. The purpose of the smash is to win the point outright.

The most obvious characteristic of the smash is the speed with which the ball is hit. But it is more important to concentrate on hitting the ball to a particular area in your opponent's court so that he will not be able to reach it. Accuracy is more essential than power. Good players can often return even the strongest smashes if they can get to the ball.

The smash is used more in doubles than in singles because the objective in doubles is to go to the net, and therefore your opponents will lob more often.

One final note. All smashes should be taken on the forehand side, even if it forces you to "run around" your backhand.

1.

1. Tom prepares to smash an oncoming lob. He has positioned himself properly and is turned with his side to the net. He has extended his left arm so that he is pointing to the ball. On the backswing he brings the racquet up instead of down, as in the serve. The racquet will fall behind his back and his swing will be similar to the uncocking of the arm in the serve.

2. Meeting the ball, Tom's arm is fully extended and his wrist snaps the racquet over in a vigorous action.

2.

3. After his wrist has snapped over, Tom starts the long follow-through while he continues to look at the ball.

———

1. As Andrea goes up for the smash, her racquet drops behind her back. Her side is to the net and she, too, sights the approaching ball by pointing to it with her left hand.

2. She reaches all the way up and her arm is uncocked. She watches the ball and sees the impact as the ball meets the center of her racquet.

3.

1.

2.

PRACTICE · HINTS · REMINDERS

Practice

Get a friend to feed you a series of lobs and practice the smash for at least twenty minutes.

At first, be satisfied to hit properly and into the court.

As you progress, hit at targets placed in the far corners of the backcourt.

Hints

See the impact.

Position yourself properly so you can make a correct swing.

Keep the ball in front of you by moving quickly.

Reminder

Although the fore-swing is the same as the serve, the back-swing is not. On the smash it is abbreviated (see text).

DOUBLES

In many ways, doubles can be a more entertaining game than singles. One advantage is that since there are two people to cover a court that is not that much wider than a singles court, it is not as demanding physically. And because there is less running to do, you are less likely to be off-balance. You can concentrate more on making your shots.

Another plus is the fun of having a partner, who is usually a friend, and the two of you can plot strategy—learning when to go to the net and when to stay back—that will carry the day. Obviously, good teamwork—knowing each other's moves and what you will do in certain situations—is essential and rewarding. Often, players who are not as good as their opponents in singles will beat them in doubles.

The volley and smash are more important strokes in doubles because they are used more frequently than in singles. The prime objective is to achieve the attacking position at the net. If you and your partner are steady volleyers, then your chances of success are greatly increased.

To return service well in doubles, you should concentrate on hitting the ball low over the net and generally back to the server. Since he will be trying to move in to join his partner at the net, aim the return at his feet, which

will force him to hit up. That will give your side a chance to volley the high return downward for a winner. Sharp, angular and more gentle volleys are preferred in doubles, rather than the deep and hard ones usually hit in singles.

Each player is responsible for his side of the court, but there are times when "poaching" is recommended. "Poaching" means to enter your partner's territory because you think you can put the ball away for a placement and win the point. But be sure, in doing so, that you gain the point and there is no return, for you have gone out of your area and left your own side vulnerable. The situation is demonstrated in the photograph below:

Serving To Forehand Court

1. Tossing the ball up, Tom starts to serve. Note that he stands approximately midway in his half of the court. His partner is positioned in the center of her half of the court but inside the service box. Her body is bent well over so she can volley any ball that may come to her.

2. Having served, Tom is coming in on the run to take a position parallel with Andrea. It is assumed that Tom has a good service and will be able to move up each time. If he has a weak service, then he shouldn't rush forward. He should stay back for one shot, take an approach shot, and then move forward to be even with his partner.

3. As the ball is about to cross the net, he continues farther in to assume his position parallel with his partner so they can work as a team on the attack and volley the return of service.

1.

2.

3.

Serving To Backhand Court

1. Tom is about to make impact with the ball because his arm is fully extended in correct serving form. Andrea is now in the left court, ready to volley the return.

2. Tom has served and is on his way in to line up with his partner so that there will be no gaps on the court. With one step he can cover the middle with a forehand; or with one step she can cover the middle with a backhand. He also can cover his alley in one step with a backhand; and she can cover her alley in one step with a forehand.

3. Tom is now in proper position. He and Andrea have built a fortress at the net and are ready to go on the attack.

1.

2.

3.

Volleying Position

1. Note that Tom and Andrea are in the center of their half of the court at equal distances from each other and from the sidelines, which include the doubles alleys.

2. The ball has been hit to Tom and he is about to make a forehand volley. He must lean away so as not to be too close to the ball.

3. The return has been hit to Andrea. She will make a forehand volley, attempting to strike the ball well out in front of her.

1.

2.

3.

Receiving Service

1. Tom is back in the forehand court to receive the service. Andrea is positioned on the service line on her side. From there she will be able to move forward with her partner when he follows in after his return.

2. Andrea is now receiving service in the backhand court, and Tom is in the proper position on the service line in his half of the court.

1.

2.

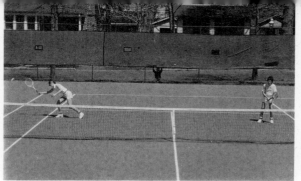

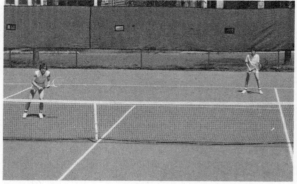

1.

Faults In Form

1. Andrea is reaching out to the alley to return the ball, but Tom has failed to move sideways to help protect the middle. This leaves a large gap in the center through which their opponents can hit the ball for a winning placement. Andrea and Tom must move together as a team.

2. Another large hole has been created because Tom is in the backcourt and Andrea is in the forecourt, making it easy for their opponents to hit between them and win the point. Tom should be opposite Andrea. When she moves in for a volley, he should, too. Conversely, they should drop back together when the situation calls for it. They should always move in tandem.

2.

PRACTICE · HINTS · REMINDERS

Practice

Practice playing doubles.

The objective is for you and your partner to form a fortress at the net and to win the points from there.

Keep the fortress intact by maintaining equal distances between you and your partner, you and your alley, and your partner and his alley.

Hints

Avoid trying to win points from the backcourt; that is your defense zone.

Get to the net before shooting for winners.

Reminder

Teamwork is the essence of good doubles.

OFFICIAL RULES OF TENNIS

The Singles Game

RULE 1
Dimensions and Equipment

The Court shall be a rectangle, 78 feet long and 27 feet wide. It shall be divided across the middle by a net, suspended from a cord or metal cable of a maximum diameter of one-third of an inch, the ends of which shall be attached to, or pass over, the tops of two posts, 3 feet 6 inches high, the center of which shall be 3 feet outside the Court on each side. The height of the net shall be 3 feet at the center, where it shall be held down taut by a strap not more than 2 inches wide. There shall be a band covering the cord or metal cable and the top of the net not less than 2 inches nor more than 2½ inches in depth on each side. The lines bounding the ends and sides of the Court shall, respectively, be called the Baselines and the Sidelines. On each side of the net, at a distance of 21 feet from it and parallel with it, shall be drawn the Service-lines. The space on each side of the net between the service-line and the sidelines shall be divided into two equal parts called the service-courts by the center service-line, which must be 2 inches in width, drawn halfway between, and parallel with, the sidelines. Each baseline shall be bisected by an imaginary continuation of the center service-line to a line 4 inches in length and 2 inches in width called the center mark drawn inside the Court, at right angles to and in contact with such baselines. All other lines shall not be less than 1 inch nor more than 2 inches in width, except the baseline, which may be 4 inches in width, and all measurements shall be made to the outside of the lines.

RULE 2
Permanent Fixtures

The permanent fixtures of the Court shall include not only the net, posts, cord or metal cable, strap and band, but also, where there are such, the back and side stops, the stands, fixed or movable seats and chairs around the Court, and their occupants, all other fixtures around and above the Court, and the Umpire, Net-cord Judge, Foot-fault Judge, Linesmen and Ball Boys when in their respective places.

RULE 3
Ball—Size, Weight and Bound

The ball shall have a uniform outer surface and shall be white or yellow in color. If there are any seams, they shall be stitchless. The ball shall be more than two and a half inches and less than two and five-eighths inches in diameter, and more than two ounces and less than two and one-sixteenth ounces in weight. The ball shall have a bound of more than 53 inches and less than 58 inches when dropped 100 inches upon a concrete base. The ball shall have a forward deformation of more than .230 of an inch and less than .290 of an inch and a return deformation of more than .355 of an inch and less than .425 of an inch at 18-pound load. The two deformation figures shall be the averages of three individual readings along three axes of the ball and no two individual readings shall differ by more than .030 of an inch in each case. All tests for bound, size and deformation shall be made in accordance with the Regulations.

RULE 4
Server and Receiver

The Players shall stand on opposite sides of the net; the player who first delivers the ball shall be called the Server, and the other the Receiver.

RULE 5
Choice of Sides and Service

The choice of sides and the right to be Server or Receiver in the first game shall be decided by toss. The player winning the toss may choose, or require his opponent to choose:

(a) The right to be Server or Receiver, in which case the other player shall choose the side; or

(b) The side, in which case the other player shall choose the right to be Server or Receiver.

RULE 6
Delivery of Service

The service shall be delivered in the following manner. Immediately before commencing to serve, the Server shall stand with both feet at rest behind (i.e., farther from the net than) the baseline, and within the imaginary continuations of the center-mark and sideline. The Server shall then project the ball by hand into the air in any direction and before it hits the ground strike it with his racquet, and the delivery shall be deemed to have been completed at the moment of the impact of the racquet and the ball. A player with the use of only one arm may utilize his racquet for the projection.

RULE 7
Foot Fault

The Server shall throughout the delivery of the service:

(a) Not change his position by walking or running.

(b) Not touch, with either foot, any area other than that behind the baseline within the imaginary extension of the center-mark and sideline.

RULE 8
From Alternate Courts

(a) In delivering the service, the Server shall stand alternately behind the right and left Courts, beginning from the right in every game. If service from a wrong half of the Court occurs and is undetected, all play resulting from such wrong service or services shall stand, but the inaccuracy of the station shall be corrected immediately it is discovered.

(b) The ball served shall pass over the net and hit the ground within the Service Court which is diagonally opposite, or upon any line bounding such Court, before the Receiver returns it.

RULE 9
Faults

The Service is a fault:

(a) If the Server commit any breach of Rules 6, 7 or 8;

(b) If he miss the ball in attempting to strike it;

(c) If the ball served touch a permanent fixture (other than the net, strap or band) before it hits the ground.

RULE 10
Service After a Fault

After a fault (if it be the first fault) the Server shall serve again from behind the same half of the Court from which he served that fault, unless the service was from the wrong half, when, in accordance with Rule 8, the Server shall be entitled to one service only from behind the other half. A fault may not be claimed after the next service has been delivered.

RULE 11
Receiver Must Be Ready

The Server shall not serve until the Receiver is ready. If the latter attempt to return the service, he shall be deemed ready. If, however, the Receiver signify that he is not ready, he may not claim a fault because the ball does not hit the ground within the limits fixed for the service.

RULE 12
A Let

In all cases where a let has to be called under the rules, or to provide for an interruption to play, it shall have the following interpretations:

(a) When called solely in respect of a service, that one service only shall be replayed.

(b) When called under any other circumstances, the point shall be replayed.

RULE 13
The Service Is a Let

The service is a let:

(a) If the ball served touch the net, strap or band, and is otherwise good, or, after touching the net, strap or band, touch the Receiver or anything which he wears or carries before hitting the ground.

(b) If a service or a fault be delivered when the Receiver is not ready (see Rule 11).

RULE 14
When Receiver Becomes Server

At the end of the first game the Receiver shall become the Server, and the Server Receiver; and so on alternately in all the subsequent games of a match. If a player serve out of turn, the player who ought to have served shall serve as soon as the mistake is discovered, but all points scored before such discovery shall be reckoned. If a game shall have been completed before such discovery, the order of service remains as altered. A fault served before such discovery shall not be reckoned.

RULE 15
Ball in Play Till Point Decided

A ball is in play from the moment at which it is delivered in service. Unless a fault or a let be called, it remains in play until the point is decided.

RULE 16
Server Wins Point

The Server wins the point:

(a) If the ball served, not being a let under Rule 13, touch the Receiver or anything which he wears or carries, before it hits the ground;

(b) If the Receiver otherwise loses the point as provided by Rule 18.

RULE 17
Receiver Wins Point

The Receiver wins the point:

(a) If the Server serve two consecutive faults;

(b) If the Server otherwise lose the point as provided by Rule 18.

RULE 18
Player Loses Point

A player loses the point if:

(a) He fail, before the ball in play has hit the ground twice consecutively, to return it directly over the net (except as provided in Rule 22 (a) or (c); or

(b) He return the ball in play so that it hits the ground, a permanent fixture, or other object, outside any of the lines which bound his opponent's Court (except as provided in Rule 22 (a) and (c); or

(c) He volley the ball and fail to make a good return even when standing outside the Court; or

(d) He touch or strike the ball in play with his racquet more than once in making a stroke; or

(e) He or his racquet (in his hand or otherwise) or anything he wears or carries touch the net, posts, cord or metal cable, strap or band, or the ground within his opponent's Court at any time while the ball is in play; or

(f) He volley the ball before it has passed the net; or

(g) The ball in play touch him or anything that he wears or carries, except his racquet in his hand or hands; or

(h) He throws his racquet at and hits the ball.

RULE 19
Player Hinders Opponent

If a player commits any act either deliberate or involuntary which, in the opinion of the Umpire, hinders his opponent in making a stroke, the Umpire shall in the first case award the point to the opponent, and in the second case order the point to be replayed.

RULE 20
Ball Falling on Line—Good

A ball falling on a line is regarded as falling in the Court bounded by that line.

RULE 21
Ball Touching Permanent Fixture

If a ball in play touch a permanent fixture (other than the net, posts, cord or metal cable, strap or band) after it has hit the ground, the player who struck it wins the point; if before it hits the ground, his opponent wins the point.

RULE 22
Good Return

It is a good return:

(a) If the ball touch the net, posts, cord or metal cable, strap or band, provided that it passes over any of them and hits the ground within the Court; or

(b) If the ball, served or returned, hit the ground within the proper Court and rebound or be blown back over the net, and the player whose turn it is to strike reach over the net and play the ball, provided that neither he nor any part of his clothes or racquet touch the net, posts, cord or metal cable, strap or band or the ground within his opponent's Court, and that the stroke be otherwise good; or

(c) If the ball be returned outside the post, either above or below the level of the top of the net, even though it touch the post, provided that it hits the ground within the proper Court; or

(d) If a player's racquet pass over the net after he has returned the ball, provided the ball pass the net before being played and be properly returned; or

(e) If a player succeeded in returning the ball, served or in play, which strikes a ball lying in the Court.

RULE 23
Interference

In case a player is hindered in making a stroke by anything not within his control except a permanent fixture of the Court, or except as provided for in Rule 19, the point shall be replayed.

RULE 24
The Game

If a player wins his first point, the score is called 15 for that player; on winning his second point, the score is called 30 for that player; on winning his third point, the score is called 40 for that player, and the fourth point won by a player is scored game for that player except as below:

If both players have won three points, the score is called deuce; and the next point won by a player is called advantage for that player. If the same player wins the next point, he wins the game; if the other player wins the next point the score is again called deuce; and so on until a player wins the two points immediately following the score at deuce, when the game is scored for that player.

RULE 25
The Set

A player (or players) who first wins six games wins a set; except that he must win by a margin of two games over his opponent and where necessary a set shall be extended until this margin be achieved.

RULE 26
When Players Change Sides

The players shall change sides at the end of the first, third and every subsequent alternate game of each set, and at the end of each set unless the total number of games in such set be even, in which case the change is not made until the end of the first game of the next set.

RULE 27
Maximum Number of Sets

The maximum number of sets in a match shall be 5, or, where women take part, 3.

RULE 28
Rules Apply to Both Sexes

Except where otherwise stated, every reference in these Rules to the masculine includes the feminine gender.

RULE 29
Decisions of Umpire and Referee

In matches where an Umpire is appointed, his decision shall be final; but where a Referee is appointed, an appeal shall lie to him from the decision of an Umpire on a question of law, and in all such cases the decision of the Referee shall be final, except that in Davis Cup matches the decision of a linesman can be changed by the Referee, or by the Umpire with the consent of the Referee.

The Referee, in his discretion, may at any time postpone a match on account of darkness or the condition of the ground or the weather. In any case of postponement the previous score and previous occupancy of Courts shall hold good, unless the Referee and the players unanimously agree otherwise.

RULE 30

Play shall be continuous from the first service till the match be concluded; provided that after the third set or when women take part, the second set, either player is entitled to a rest, which shall not exceed 10 minutes, or in countries situated between Latitude 15 degrees North and Latitude 15 degrees South, 45 minutes, and provided further that when necessitated by circumstances not within the control of the players, the Umpire may suspend play for such a period as he may consider necessary. If play be suspended and be not resumed until a later day, the rest may be taken only after the third set (or when women take part the second set) of play on such later day, completion of an unfinished set being counted as one set. These provisions shall be strictly construed, and play shall never be suspended, delayed or interfered with for the purpose of enabling a player to recover his strength or his wind, or to

receive instruction or advice. The Umpire shall be the sole judge of such suspension, delay or interference, and after giving due warning he may disqualify the offender.

(a) Any nation is at liberty to modify the first provision of Rule 30, or omit it from its regulations governing tournaments, matches, or competitions held in its own country, other than the International Lawn Tennis Championships (Davis Cup and Federation Cup).

(b) When changing sides, a maximum of one minute shall elapse from the cessation of the previous game to the time players are ready to begin the next game.

The Doubles Game

RULE 31

The above Rules shall apply to the Doubles Game except as below.

RULE 32
Dimensions of Court

For the Doubles Game, the Court shall be 36 feet in width, i.e., 4½ feet wider on each side than the Court for the Singles Game, and those portions of the singles sidelines which lie between the two service-lines shall be called the service sidelines. In other respects, the Court shall be similar to that described in Rule 1, but the portions of the singles sidelines between the baseline and service-line on each side of the net may be omitted if desired.

RULE 33
Order of Service

The order of serving shall be decided at the beginning of each set as follows:

The pair who have to serve in the first game of each set shall decide which partner shall do so and the opposing pair shall decide similarly for the second game. The partner of the player who served in the first game shall serve in the third; the partner of the player who served in the second game shall serve in the fourth, and so on in the same order in all the subsequent games of a set.

RULE 34
Order of Receiving

The order of receiving the service shall be decided at the beginning of each set as follows:

The pair who have to receive the service in the first game shall decide which partner shall receive the first service, and that partner shall continue to receive the first service in every odd game throughout that set. The opposing pair shall likewise decide which partner shall receive the first service in the second game and that partner shall continue to receive the first service in every even game throughout that set. Partners shall receive the service alternately throughout each game.

RULE 35
Service Out of Turn

If a partner serve out of his turn, the partner who ought to have served shall serve as soon as the mistake is discovered, but all points scored, and any faults served before such discovery shall be reckoned. If a game shall have been completed before such discovery, the order of service remains as altered.

RULE 36
Error in Order of Receiving

If during a game the order of receiving the service is changed by the receivers it shall remain as altered until the end of the game in which the mistake is discovered, but the partners shall resume their original order of receiving in the next game of that set in which they are receivers of the service.

RULE 37
Ball Touching Server's Partner Is Fault

The service is a fault as provided for by Rule 9, or if the ball served touch the Server's partner or anything he wears or carries; but if the ball served touch the partner of the Receiver or anything which he wears or carries, not being a let under Rule 13 (a), before it hits the ground, the Server wins the point.

RULE 38
Ball Struck Alternately

The ball shall be struck alternately by one or other player of the opposing pairs, and if a player touches the ball in play with his racquet in contravention of this Rule, his opponents win the point.

(Rules reprinted by permission of the United States Lawn Tennis Association)